ASTROLOGY

VIRGO

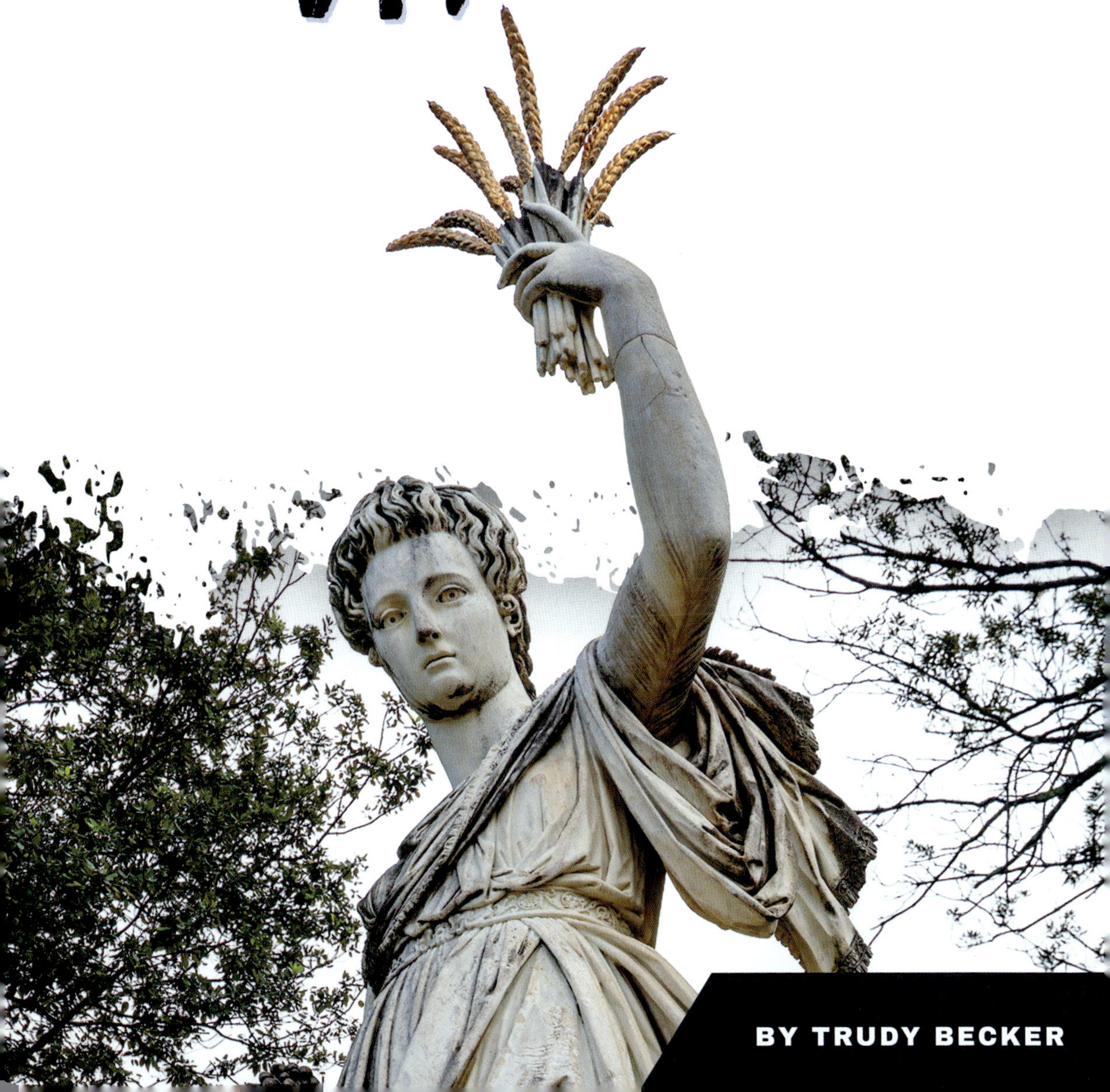

BY TRUDY BECKER

Apex is distributed by North Star Editions:
sales@northstareditions.com | 888-417-0195

Produced for Apex by Red Line Editorial.

Photographs ©: Shutterstock Images, cover (illustration, constellation), cover (background), 1, 4–5, 7, 9, 10–11, 12–13, 14, 16–17, 18–19, 20, 21, 22–23, 25, 26, 27, 29; CM Dixon/Print Collector/Hulton Archive/Getty Images, 8

Library of Congress Control Number: 2025939157

ISBN
979-8-89250-791-2 (hardcover)
979-8-89250-820-9 (paperback)
979-8-89250-877-3 (ebook pdf)
979-8-89250-849-0 (hosted ebook)

Printed in the United States of America
Mankato, MN
012026

NOTE TO PARENTS AND EDUCATORS

Apex books are designed to build literacy skills in striving readers. Exciting, high-interest content attracts and holds readers' attention. The text is carefully leveled to allow students to achieve success quickly. Additional features, such as bolded glossary words for difficult terms, help build comprehension.

TABLE OF CONTENTS

CHAPTER 1

THE CONSTELLATION

Virgo is a **constellation**. Four of its stars make a box shape. Other stars form several bent lines.

VIRGO

Virgo is one of the largest constellations in the night sky.

For many years, people have said these stars look like a woman. For example, the Romans linked the constellation to Ceres. She was a goddess of **agriculture**.

FAST FACT

Virgo's brightest star is called Spica. That is Latin for "ear of grain."

The Romans believed Ceres helped plants grow. She is often shown holding wheat.

People throughout the Middle East worshipped Ishtar. She sometimes had ties to rain or growing plants.

Ancient Babylonians linked Virgo to Ishtar. She was a goddess of love and war.

BRINGING SPRING

The ancient Greeks linked Virgo to Persephone. She was a goddess. The Greeks said she went to the underworld for part of each year. When she came back to Earth, spring started.

Stories say Persephone ate pomegranate seeds while in the underworld. And because she ate food there, she had to stay.

CHAPTER 2

THE ZODIAC SIGN

Virgo is part of the **zodiac**. The zodiac divides the year into 12 parts. Each part, or sign, is based on a constellation. Virgo is the sixth sign.

The signs of the zodiac are often shown in a wheel. They start with Aries and go counterclockwise.

Virgo's time starts around August 23. It lasts until about September 22. People born during this time have Virgo as their **sun sign**.

FAST FACT

Virgo is a mutable sign. That means its time comes at the end of a season.

Virgo is paired with the time when summer turns into fall. The new season can bring changes, such as the start of school.

Astrology claims that signs shape how people think and act. For example, Virgos are said to be good at thinking and planning.

RISING VIRGO

In astrology, each person has several signs. Their rising sign comes from the time of day they were born. Having Virgo as a rising sign is said to make people calm and **reliable**.

Virgos often enjoy jobs in health care or other fields that involve keeping track of many details.

CHAPTER 3

ABOUT VIRGO

Each zodiac sign has a **glyph**. Virgo's looks similar to an M. But it has an added loop.

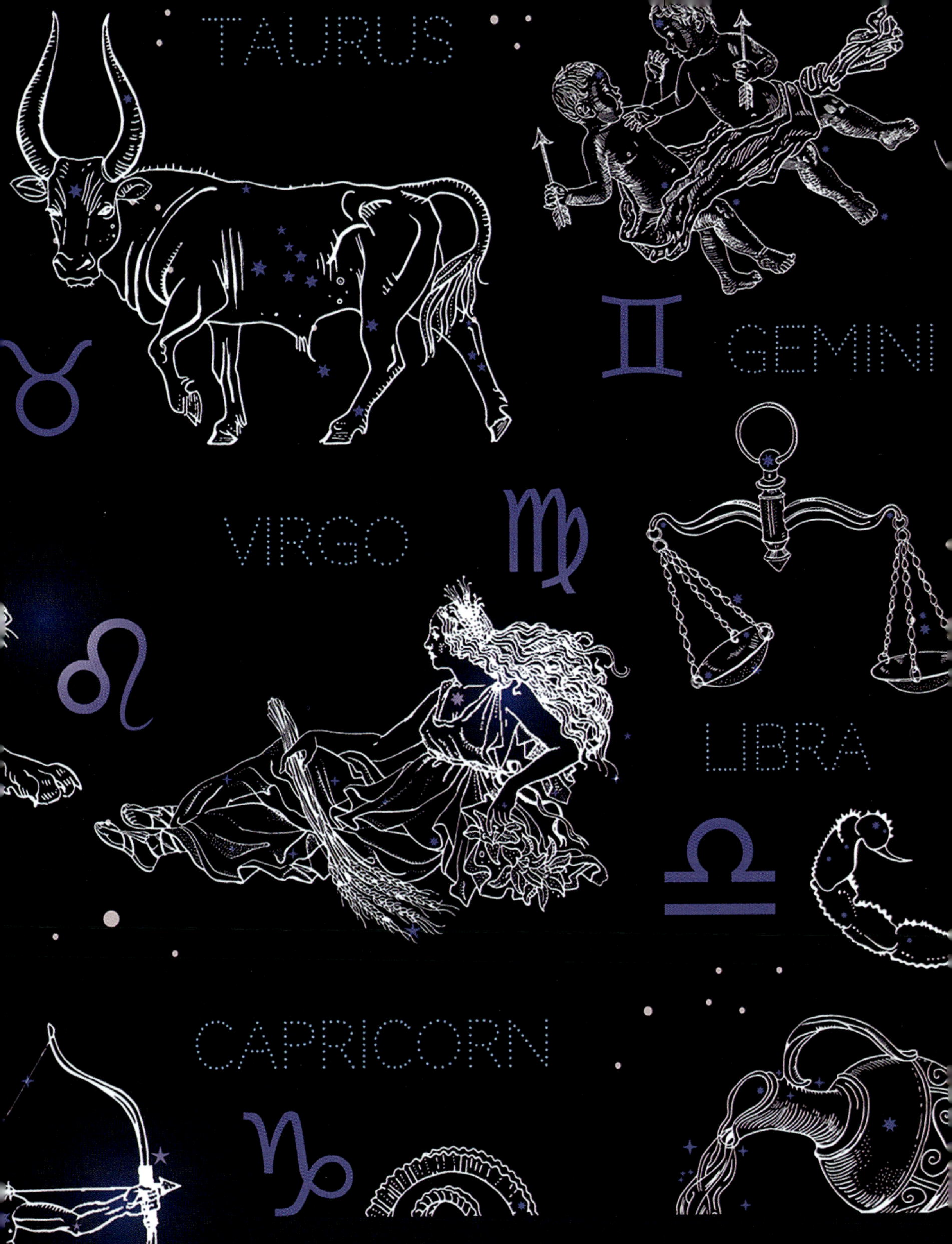

As well as a glyph, each zodiac sign has a person, object, or animal that represents it. Virgo's is a girl.

Virgo's **element** is earth. Earth signs are said to be practical and realistic. And many Virgos are good at solving problems.

Many Virgos enjoy growing food or flowers in a garden.

FAST FACT

Change is hard for some earth signs. But Virgos often work to make things better.

Mercury is named for a Roman god who was a messenger.

Virgo's ruling planet is Mercury. In astrology, Mercury is the planet of **communication**. It's said to help Virgos explain things. They may be good at writing, too.

SHARING A PLANET

Mercury is the ruling planet for both Virgo and Gemini. It's said to affect each sign differently. It makes Virgos great at taking in information. And it helps Geminis express themselves.

Virgos often like learning a lot about one topic.

CHAPTER 4

SOLVING PROBLEMS

Virgos are often described as skilled organizers. They can break big ideas into small steps. Then they help make sure each step goes smoothly.

Virgos are good at noticing details that others might miss.

Virgos are also known for working hard. They try to do everything exactly the right way. And they tend to be very good at what they do.

FAST FACT

Famous Virgos include Beyoncé, Patrick Mahomes, and Zendaya.

Zendaya is world-famous for both her acting and her sense of style. ▶

Virgos often use their skills to help others. Friends and family can count on them to help fix problems. Virgos also tend to give good advice.

Being a teacher can be a good job for a Virgo.

Virgos may feel upset if things don't go as planned.

PERFECTIONISTS

Some Virgos are perfectionists. They can be hard on themselves or others. It's important for them to remember that no one is perfect. Mistakes and problems are normal parts of life.

COMPREHENSION QUESTIONS

Write your answers on a separate piece of paper.

1. Write a few sentences describing the main ideas of Chapter 3.

2. Do you find it easy to pay close attention to details? Why or why not?

3. Which sign in the zodiac is Virgo?

A. the first sign
B. the sixth sign
C. the twelfth sign

4. According to astrology, what type of job would Virgos like best?

A. a job where they could solve problems
B. a job where they don't have to learn new things
C. a job where nothing ever changes

5. What does **affect** mean in this book?

It's said to ***affect*** *each sign differently. It makes Virgos great at taking in information. And it helps Geminis express themselves.*

- **A.** stop something from happening
- **B.** take the place of something
- **C.** shape what something is like

6. What does **organizers** mean in this book?

Virgos are often described as skilled ***organizers****. They can break big ideas into small steps.*

- **A.** tools that hold papers
- **B.** people who make plans
- **C.** people who don't plan

Answer key on page 32.

GLOSSARY

agriculture

Growing plants or raising animals to sell or use as food.

communication

Sending and receiving messages.

constellation

A group of stars that form a shape.

element

One of four forces (air, earth, fire, or water) that each zodiac sign is matched with and said to be shaped by.

glyph

A shape that stands for a word or idea.

reliable

Able to be counted on.

sun sign

A person's main zodiac sign, which is decided by the date they were born.

zodiac

The set of 12 signs used in astrology, based on a part of the sky that the sun appears to move through each year.

TO LEARN MORE

BOOKS

Andrews, Elizabeth. *The Ancient Greeks*. Abdo Publishing, 2023.

Goldstein, Margaret J. *Mysteries of Stars*. Lerner Publications, 2021.

McMullen, Gemma. *The Stars*. Little Blue House, 2025.

ONLINE RESOURCES

Visit **www.apexeditions.com** to find links and resources related to this title.

ABOUT THE AUTHOR

Trudy Becker lives in Minneapolis, Minnesota. She likes exploring new places and loves anything involving books.

INDEX

ANSWER KEY:
1. Answers will vary; 2. Answers will vary; 3. B; 4. A; 5. C; 6. B